Mental Models

Mental models: tools of thought that separate the average from the exceptional. Better decisions, clearer thinking and greater self-awareness.

Table of Contents

Furthermore, the transmission, duplication, or reproduction of any of the following work including specific information will be considered an illegal act irrespective of if it is done electronically or in print. This extends to creating a secondary or tertiary copy of the work or a recorded copy and is only allowed with the express written consent from the Publisher. All additional right reserved.

The information in the following pages is broadly considered a truthful and accurate account of facts and as such, any inattention, use, or misuse of the information in question by the reader will render any resulting actions solely under their purview. There are no scenarios in which the publisher or the original author of this work can be in any fashion deemed liable for any hardship or damages that may befall them after undertaking information described herein.

Additionally, the information in the following pages is intended only for informational purposes and should thus be thought of as universal. As befitting its nature, it is presented without assurance regarding its prolonged validity or interim quality. Trademarks that are mentioned are done without written consent and can in no way be considered an endorsement from the trademark holder.

Introduction

"Two heads are better than one," many people say. It's no surprise because our own biases and experiences limit us. We also lack the areas of expertise, which results in the development and priority of mental models that you might not realize in the first place.

For example, there are two employees. The first one excels in sales while the latter remains superb in other business aspects. When both of them work together, their combined insights can crack a challenge. However, it's not always possible to host a discussion when making a crucial decision. As a professional, it's important to think about the problem yourself. But the good news is that there's an excellent way to maximize your decision-making, commonly called mental models.

You probably have heard it before. But what is a mental model? How can you navigate your mental model? Good questions. You have come to the right place! In this eBook, you will know everything about mental modes! Are you ready? Take a close look at the following.

Chapter 1: Decision-Making Ability and the Basics

The process of decision-making is selecting among two or more courses of the deed for a particular scenario. Deciding a crucial part of our day-to-day life. A few think of it as an art, some think of it as a proficiency. Your decisions might be expert or individual. Whatever the case, your options will have lasting effects.

In short, the decisions you make have the chance to impact yourself and other people both temporarily and continuously. Thus, you must acquire the necessary skill set, which will enable you to weigh and reflect your choices. You must choose the best decision, which will be most suitable for every scenario.

Laymen and professionals equally have presented a numerous recommendations about how to become a proficient decision-maker. A few support an elementary method, like establishing a mental checklist referred to when a person is confronted with options. A few want to execute a complicated set of processes, which must end in best results.

Determine the Concern or Goal that Needs a Decision

The initial step is to determine the decision which you're experiencing. The issue might be easy enough to talk about with basic language, not needing hours of refection.

You need to bear in mind that decision-making isn't connected to an issue. However, it could take the form of goal setting as well. For example, you might be considering about your future, and you say to yourself, *"Going to university is possibly a great choice if I like to make lots of money in the future."* Here, your goal is obvious, even though this is addressed quite innocently.

One way that similar goal could be explained might be with more urbane redundancy like this one: *"I am challenged with the decision of going to college and delaying employment or seeking a work and participating the workforce as soon as possible."* You see, those are the options, which need higher exploration.

Always remember that no matter how your goal or issue is determined; the essential point is the initial step within your decision-making process. You need to state your problem in an understandable and plain language.

Collect Data and Alternatives Linked with Options

You have now a clear idea in mind of the decision you are experiencing. The next step is to research every possible option you have. This will vary greatly on the seriousness of the problem you are suffering, and the fastness the decision should be made.

In the scenario of life choice about attending college, that's a decision, which will need higher research and thought. Relevant data should be collected before determination. You must always keep in mind that this stage also covers looking asking some advice from people in the field as well as the opinions of your trusted friends and family members. Their experience might offer you with practical and valuable insight, which would progress the process.

Ultimately, a gathering of information will lead to the determination of options for every preference. You must integrate those findings into the step of gathering information.

Decide

After the alternatives have been sightseen comprehensively, and you have already a list of options, what's next? It is time that you choose one of the options which have been created. Choosing the ideal solution isn't as simple as it might look. But the real process of making the decision on an alternative will be easier. That's true, particularly if you have put in the dedication and effort to determine the problem and explore your options. That will enable you to move forward with higher self-confidence.

In the example where a young man is considering the benefits and drawbacks of college attendance, you will find different options. Maybe, he could attend college part-time and work part-time at the same time. Perhaps, he can attend a less costly college, allowing him to free up some money for relocating out of the home. In this case, you will find a wide array of options. Thus, the consequences of decision-making are a bit complicated.

It's also the time where a preference should be designated. It's the part in the decision-making process, which could trigger stress. It needs a leap of trust, a level of instinctive instinct, as well as personal understanding. If the person has used enough effort, it will enable him to choose the perfect decision with much confidence.

It's also suggested that even when a decision has been decided, the personal challenged with the task must take time to think. It would be ideal to allow the subconscious mind to do the entire thinking. In short, you have executed the decision-making process to that point. You have already determined the issue, you have also considered the options accessible, and you've made a rational decision according to the data you gathered.

It's time to have faith in yourself to suppress the decision. Pay attention carefully to your internal voice.

Put your Decision into Action and Assess

It's not typical for individuals to postpone their decision making only because they're uncertain about making life-defining decisions. However, that's part of becoming an adult. Every time you implement that process, you also become more competent and adept in the skill. You become more assured of your own ability to use it for your own gain.

Whatever decision you are challenged with making, you need to act on it later on. You will find an exhilarating sensation, which comes with action. Especially if it's based on the right application of the process of decision-making.

The young man who's trying to make the decision whether or not to attend college has decided that he'll require an advanced education if he likes to participate in the work setting. He has limited funds but doesn't prefer to live at home. Therefore, he decided to enroll in a close community college. He also discovered a full-time employment, and he is relocating into a good apartment close to his school.

The decision maker in the example we presented is happy with his decisions. He is always more content with his capability to manipulate the process of decision-making to his gain. Through the following weeks or months, he will assess the decisions he has made to identify if it's the best option for his case. He will also determine whether the plan should be adjusted in some manner.

The presentation of the decision-making process has improved his skills in the steps, which are needed to steer the choices of life.

Are you currently trying into this study? Do you like to become a more skillful individual, if not expert? When we talk about decision-making, it's relevant to keep in mind the four basic steps of the process.

Make sure that you state the problem first in a plain and clear language. Next, do all your research on every option accessible to handle the issue. Then, you need to make the decision from the alternatives measured. Finally, ratify the decision and assess to make sure that it's a suitable one to reach its specified purpose.

Take note that practice always makes perfect. That's basically significant when we talk about decision-making.

Chapter 2: Deal with Conflict

Every time you are surrounded by people, there will always be a conflict. Opinions always differ, and misunderstandings and miscommunications take place. Individuals have unique urgencies and standards in their lives, and the majority battles change.

All of those establish conflict in everyone's work and life. The issue is not the conflict itself. It is how people deal with it. Fortunately, having efficient conflict management approach could be understood and mastered easily. In this section, allow us to present some tips on how you can efficiently handle interpersonal conflict.

- **Stay away from troublemakers**

This type of people will only suck you in and drag you all the way down. We encourage that you do not interact in backstabbing or any type of gossip. You must get the facts properly before you shift to conclusions about something you heard through the branches.

You must be aware of when it is time to walk away from a confrontation. Consider always the main source in the face of upsetting comments or criticisms.

- **Improve your communication skills**

The skill to communicate yourself openly will enable you to tell what is on your mind. It also enables you to request what you need and want, as well as helping you get your point across. You might be familiar with the maxim that a problem well specified is a problem half-resolved.

- **Work to lessen conflict**

  You need to take the necessary steps to lessen conflict at work before it takes place. Work at establishing good relationships along with colleagues and coworkers. You must get to know other people as well. You need to become sociable and friendly too.

  Keep in mind that everybody has various priorities and needs. They also come from various cultural backgrounds. As opposed to what you normally have heard, familiarity breeds respect.

- **Pick your battles**

  You will always find various opinions and ways of doing stuff. Make the decision to which problems you could live and determine which of them need dealing with. You will establish credibility if you know how to bring only the most vital problems. Meanwhile, you will be named a complainer if you make an issue about all thing.

- **Say sorry when suitable**

  You need to become mindful of your own part when establishing the conflict. Have you ever done something wrong or not appropriate? Then, it's suitable that you acknowledge and say to others that you are sorry. That's right even when the conflict is not an outcome of your actions. Often, you will have to meet people in the middle to get where you wish to go.

- **Take advantage of a mediator if needed**

  Do your efforts haven't worked the way you want it? Then you can invite a neutral third party when the situation is worrying or instable. You can invite a supervisor to serve as an intermediary if it's amenable to everyone concerned.

  That person could remain objectively, listen to every party, and simplify resolution and cooperation. You must be firm on your goals. Remember that you are there to fix a conflict and not to reverse an enemy.

- **Discuss it personally**

Let's face it; meeting in person is always intimidating. However, it is often the ideal option to go. You see, direct communication is much efficient than other types, as it enables for an active exchange of data. It also offers you the chance to utilize hand gestures, eye contact, smile, handshake, and other types of body language.

That enables you to perceive vital non-verbal signals from the other side. You need to set aside some time to meet along with the other individual personally at a convenient place and time. Instead of meeting on one of your offices, ensure you meet on a "neutral turf."

Furthermore, writing of a letter, messaging, social media, and email must be prevented. Doing this will prevent talking about sensitive topics, problems, and hurting other's feelings. Take note that it's not direct and impersonal when you use these mediums. You also raise the risk of misunderstanding and miscommunication. A phone call would be your next option if the in-person meetings were not feasible.

- **Handle it**

The majority of individuals want to stay away from conflict. In fact, some people have actually quit their work instead of trying to fix an interpersonal conflict at their work. But it's never a good answer, as it normally results in feelings of guilt and regret. Aside from that, you will be just quitting your work in a short period if you quit whenever you have a conflict with your work. Every conflict should be handled appropriately. If you just ignore and stay away from it, it could result in raised stress. It might also present unresolved feelings of resentment, hostility, and anger. You will be healthier and happier in your life if you learn how to handle your conflict efficiently.

You will have a wonderful relationship with other people. You will become a better leader at work, a better member of the team, and a better individual in general. You will earn respect, boost your confidence, and establish your courage.

- **Contemplate it through**

    You need to consider talking about the situation with an impartial family member or friend before you address the other person with whom you have a conflict. Doing this could help you clarify needs and problems. Search for advice and feedback whenever you deal with the situation.

    However, you must always be watchful not to depend on the opinion of an involved third party. That's because this person might have his or her own goal. You need to plan your strategy very carefully. Device what you wish to say and write it down. Rehearse it if needed.

    You can also make a notecard along with your key talking points. That will guide you to feel more in control and stay on your target.

When you're able to lead other people, conflict is sure to arise. In a workgroup, critical conversations on tasks and direction sometimes draw out competing concepts. Various differences rooting from diversity and diverse perspectives also add. The capability to work efficiently through and fix conflict sometimes determines a high performing work group from one, which fails to do.

One of the advantages of conflict resolution is that it improves the assurance among conflict friends. Dealing over the conflict, along with other people, ties the conflict partner as they encounter issues and deal with the trials organized. Moreover, it gets the involved individuals in the conflict discerning in terms of "we" rather than "me." That improves the dedication of both parties to the process of conflict resolution.

Choice quality is enhanced when ideas are vetted. Flaws, which might have been ignored if people prevent talking about the problem are seen, and optimal solutions are created. If you have taken apart in this argument, you are more likely to support the execution of a specific solution, although it might not be your preferred option. That's because you have felt their ideas have been considered and that you've been involved in searching for an answer.

Chapter 3: Unlock People Potential

You and everyone is born in the world with a spotless slate. The similar unlimited potential. However, when you go to other ends, it might look that a few have been gifted with more potential than other people have. The reason behind this is that you go through your journey of life. You establish limitations and boundaries on yourself.

Many of those started way back when you are a young kid. It's when you are still a sponge, who is willing and is craving to absorb information of the world around you and the world beyond you. You depended mostly on your parents, your sibling, and your close family. Later on, you widened to your friend's teachers, and far along with relationships at work.

Throughout those vital development phases, you are imprinted with the values and belief of such individuals. You mostly based the majority of your values and beliefs on such foundations.

Unluckily, as young kids, you are often told, *"You aren't intelligent!"* *"You won't be worthy at anything you do!"* *"You are a loser"* and other stuff. When those phrases come from the individuals you trust and respect the most, you then believe it. Once those sorts of beliefs are brought through life, your esteem, self-confidence, and potential reduce.

Therefore, if you're currently on a point on your mission that you believe you could do more, or become more, below are some of the stuff you could to change your thinking:

1. **No excuses**

   You must stick with every change you decide. We understand that change could be difficult, particularly when doing the stuff you have not done before. That denotes establishing new habits, which will be not comfortable on you, part. Plan your next day every night. Think of the things you need to be completed and how do you plan to do it. Remember, the least sum of disclosures you have every day is going to stop you from being sidetracked. You also need to get into every day along with a hundred percent attitude.

We know that change could sometimes be difficult. However, as long as you create a decision to transform, you will be on your way. Prefer to learn. Transform into a much positive internal language. Adopt every challenge throughout the way. Be stimulated by the challenges. If you need some assistance, go for it.

2. Believe you always can

As we stated earlier, most of your beliefs were imprinted when you are still a kid. We acquired them, and you could *'unlearn'* them if you want. From there, new and fresh values could be established. Once you do this, your unconscious mind will work along with them. That will help you establish results, which will be dependable to them.

These days, you will come across different individuals who will judge and criticize you to who you are. They will do what they can just to cut you down, but that's all right. These people do not have similar values and beliefs as you, nor do they perceive the same image as you. Therefore, be focused on your journey without walking on to theirs.

3. Establish an image

You must understand what you truly desire if you like to make some changes. Ask yourself, *"What is my true potential?" "What does it look?" What am I doing in the picture?"* You must let yourself sense the feelings and hear the sounds.

You will have no idea of what you're striving if you do not picture your result. It does not matter what image is suitable today, as it could change in the future. What's important is that you have something to start.

4. Develop your mindset

Some individuals live with a Fixed Mindset. These individuals think that their intellect, potential as well as a character, is outlined and established after they are born. On the other hand, individuals with a Growth Mindset think that their intellect, potential as well as character could be enhanced.

They also think that everyone is born with a clean slate. Each individual in this world could be whatever he or she likes to be. They choose to enhance their life situation by understanding and adopting themselves and by failing.

You must distinguish such two mindsets and make sure you have the latter. It's vital as well that you decide to change it if you think your mindset belongs to the Fixed.

5. Accept who you truly are as a person

You can establish a vision of moving forward by understanding where your life is and approving you are where you always meant to be. Do you feel life indebted you for your past? Then you're just waiting for it to be presented to you. That will take you a very long period.

Indeed, a few events in your life might not have been fair to you. Some of them might have hurt you, and some might have been totally wrong. Nevertheless, if you will hold onto those and emotions are connected to them; that will only keep you where you are today. Learn to accept where you are now and decide to change.

Few individuals think that we are here in the world for a reason, a particular purpose. Some think they are here only because they are, without a given goal. No matter where you fit on that scale is just fine. Irrespective of where that is, you must aim to be the best version of you that you could possibly be. That's what truly means of living to your real potential.

Use these strategies above to unlock your potential and help others to unlock their potential as well. As leaders, you create an impact each day on the people around you. It is your decision, whether it is a good one or not. Assisting other people to unlock their own potential is the best gift you can offer them. Take the time to assist other people to grow and learn. You will be surprised at what could take place once you release their potential. Who knows, it might just beginning a chain reaction of development.

Chapter 4: How Avoidance Breeds Success

Each of us has our own desires, aims, and drives in lives that we wish to accomplish. However, the majority of individuals do not consider the *"strings attached"* to the difficult journey they are beginning. For that reason, we sometimes experience lots of emotional and mental failure, resulting in a downward shift in your action, confidence, and willpower.

These might come as a huge surprise to you. After all, every one of us has been refined to study very hard since we were children, top every exam and receive that diploma. All of those to accomplish the bet goal to become successful.

Avoid direct goals

That typically agreed guidance is famous when you feel dazed with your life. This could be either at work or at home. That takes place when trials and stuff you like are the decision of others. It might be your wife or husband, your manager, and in other cases, your kid.

Everything exerts some sort of control over you and your life. What is the reason why you must avoid direct goals?

The concern with the assistance of concentrating on what you could govern is that it could result as if not anything is under your control. Especially when the things you cannot control are the most vital in your life. Breaking down the emotional fences of your loved ones, having time for yourself, getting a raise – have an impact on what you cannot control.

It is better if you achieve indirect goals rather than setting direct goals. An indirect goal is when your decisions and direct behaviors impact the activities as well as the decision making of others. The effect of anything indirect is not measurable.

For instance, visualize a dartboard. Your aim is to hit the goal. Well, that's a good example of a direct goal. You perform a direct action, which is tossing the dart. You could also notice the outcome of that direct action – the location of the dart when it hits. You amend your toss and try another. You can perform that as long as required to accomplish the direct goal.

Then, turn the lights off now. It is total black. How can you hit the goal? Try to throw your dart. You could probably hear where your dart lands, but you cannot see how close you are to the target. It is also not possible to make some adjustments. All you could do is toss where you believe the bullseye might be and have some faith that you hit the mark. That's how it feels overlooking the things you do not have control. Sounds difficult, right? That's where indirect goals enter.

Visualize that you can to turn on a light after every toss. You could check where your previous dart landed. You could then arrange the following throw before the light turns off once more. It is still much difficult to hit the board if the light is turned on. However, that's much better than not having any lights to help you. That kind of method is known as "shining a light" on the outcomes. It rearranges according to what you could tell. Retrying is a thought of accomplishing things you like even if you do not have control over it.

It will take you some patience and time to accomplish an indirect goal. But it will surely pay off in the long run.

Avoid thinking like an expert

Nowadays, it appears as if everybody is an expert at everything. From your co-worker to your old classmate, everybody you know is an expert at anything they recently obtained.

For instance, a "mom bod" drops 30 pounds in just 2 months and posts her results on Facebook, Instagram, and other platforms and – viola! – we have another health expert accommodating applications for training customers.

Another example would be, a businessperson makes some great decisions. Then suddenly, he becomes a "business coach" to keen viewers, prepared to make it huge. You see, everybody becomes an expert nowadays. Nevertheless, they are not really.

Take note that expertise does not denote you know more than your friends about a particular subject. It denotes you are informed more than the majority of people about a particular subject. It denotes you have understood your arena and that you have spent long hours of learning your skills before you start informing someone on how to do it. That also means that you have performed all the work.

You need to bear in mind that it does not mean you cannot share your work with other people. What it truly means is that you cannot exercise it in a public way that is both humble and honest, helping other people as you go. It only denotes you should not throw around words such as *"expert."*

We are not trying to shock you from assisting anyone with your own experience and sharing what you have already obtained from life. We only need to be cautious about how you position yourself. Perhaps, you must stop calling yourself and thinking like an expert. Instead, start thinking like you're a student.

The world does not need more and more experts. What we truly need are learners. The world requires a group of individuals who is happy to learn their own expertise for 10 years before they begin a blog teaching others how to perform it. The world requires students, and not endless numbers of teachers. The world requires more doers and fewer talkers.

You must be careful right there. An individual isn't an expert only because they think and say they are. Take note that *expert* is only a label you gain only when other individuals notice you are doing something the same thing over again; that's the time they'll start to cry it out on your behalf.

Only because you did something on one occasion does not make you the expert on that topic. It only denotes you lived through an experience that is effective but does not make you become an expert.

Avoid to-do Lists

No matter if you are a keen supporter of a to-do list or you are a hating list-maker, the majority of us keep one. However, your to-do lists somewhat overwhelm and frustrate.

You see, you always overload your list. Social psychologists tell that one individual has approximately 150 various tasks at a time. A CEO's to-do list for one day could take more than one week to complete. Another research claims how comprehensive planning works if you have one huge to-do task. Simply put, the longer the list of your goals and tasks, the less powerful a tool of this to-do list becomes.

You need to bear in mind that overstuffing your list triggers a tenacious thrum of anxiety in your head. That will only obstruct you from handling every working task. It is also found out that stress that comes from having many contradictory goals results in your productivity, mental and physical health to suffer.

Your to-do list helps your recall different things you need to deal within a day or a week. However, it is also a nagging tool, which could trigger risky and disarming stress to your body.

While a to-do list is helpful for organization of your task, they are not the best tool for your productivity issues. As an alternative, you can convert them to *done list.* Did you know that jotting down what you achieve increases the insight and encouragement, which balances out the shortcomings and issues of your to-do list?

The boost you receive from having a visible track record drives you to handle what is next while failing to determine how much you do makes it simple to lose perspective. Your brainpower and time are too important to spend on thinking about everything you must be doing. As an alternative, seek balance and wisdom from recognizing the authenticity of your achievements.

Avoid the path of least resistance

The journey of least resistance is a truth of nature. The rivers move around the mountain instead of flowing through it. The electricity flows through the simplest route. Unluckily, our human nature is the same.

Human beings are more likely to do what is the simplest. Occasionally, we ignore what is best. For instance, it is much simpler to lose our temper with our partner than to control it. It is much simpler to sit in front of the television rather than spending our time with our children. It is much simpler to read a magazine instead of reading the Bible.

Succeeding the path of least resistant could turn out to be a habit, helping guide our lives. Most of the time, we make choices according to what is least hurting, most enjoyable, and simplest.

Bear this in mind: the secret to success depends on the very thing you are avoiding. Such things appear to break you down and shy your spirit. Search for discomfort. You must become unhurried about doing other stuff, which pushes your limits remarkably.

Difficulty helps you grow as a person. If you are seeking for long-term success, you must stop preventing what is hard and start embracing it. You are not comfortable if you are driving yourself to advance.

Every time you are challenged, you are obliged to be more than you are. That simply denotes establishing new viewpoints, obtaining new abilities, and pushing boundaries. In short, you need to widen your comprehension to surpass the challenges you are experiencing. Learning to become at ease with uneasiness is one of the vital abilities you could have to live a satisfying life. You could master nearly anything once you learn that skill.

One thing you could do is to break the chain of simple routines. Start reading a book you typically disregard. Search and listen to music from those inexperienced composers. You can also participate in workshops or events you have been disregarding. Start that complicated discussion with your officemate at work.

You must not hang out along with the similar individuals who share the same perspective, beliefs, and tastes just like you do. Start getting to know somebody who has a different background. Stepping up when it is painful or annoying establishes your character. Learn how to make time on what really matters to you. Always avoid the path of least resistance.

Chapter 5: The Murphy Law

Are you the kind of individual who thinks that anything which could go wrong, will go wrong when you least anticipate it, at the worst possible time? If yes, you are existing under the power of *Murphy's Law.*

The majority of individuals will understand this law as a negative perception of life. They could not be far from reality. Remember that Murphy's Law is designed under the robust values of forward-thinking and organizing efficient possibility plans, which will help defend against potential hindrances. It lessens the negative effect of the obstructions, which lay before you.

This law catches your imagination. Murphy's Law, as well as its offshoots, has been gathered in web sites and books. Various brands are also named after this law, and it's a sought-after name for many taverns and Irish pubs all across the globe.

However, you must understand that Murphy's Law is a new idea, which dates back in the mid of the previous century. The magician Adam Hull Shirk wrote in his essay that in a particular magic act, 9 out of ten things could go wrong. Before that, it was referred to as the *Sod's Law,* telling that any unfortunate thing could take place to poor sod will. Murphy's Law is still called *Sod's Law* in the country of England.

Origins of the Murphy's Law

Have you heard of Edward J. Murphy? Unbelievably, he was a real individual. He was a major in the United State Air Force in the 1940s who specializes in development engineering. Murphy's work was involved mainly in testing experimental designs, and he was challenged with stuff that did not go to plan. Scholars vary on what words were utilized originally when the phrase *Murphy's Law* was initially invented. Still, the meaning is crystal clear.

Murphy and his crew were breaking new ground. They were not able to depend on the type of proven methods employed efficiently elsewhere in the military to guarantee zero defects. Therefore, they need to rely on their own resourcefulness to get things done.

In 1949, officers were doing project MX981 tests to know how many Gs *(the force of gravity)* a human could endure. They believed that their conclusions could be used to design future airplanes.

The team then utilizes a rocket known as the *Gee Whiz*. That will enable them to fuel the fire of the airplane smash. The sled traveled over two hundred miles every hour down. It comes to a sudden halt in less than a second. The only concern is that the team should have an individual who will experience how much force a person could endure.

That's where Colonel John Paul Stapp comes in. Stapp was a career physician for the Air Force who steps up to try the rocket sled. Throughout various months, Stapp took a ride after punishing journey. He was imperiled to destroyed vessels in the eyes, concussions, wrecked bones, just for the sake of science.

Murphy also participated in one of the tests. He has a set of sensors, which could be used to the harness. Such sensors can calculate the exact quantity of G-force applied once the rocket sled break.

The initial trial after Murphy hanged up his sensors to the harness generated no reading. That's because every sensor had been connected inappropriately. For every sensor, there are two different ways of linking them. He found out that every sensor was installed incorrectly.

After Murphy found out the error, he complained something about the operator who was accused of the mishap. Murphy said that if there are two different ways to perform something, and one of such were led in disaster; the person would do it that way.

Murphy immediately goes back to Wright Airfield where he was posted after that incident. However, Stapp determined the universality of what Murphy had stated. In a press conference, Stapp said that the good safety record of the rocket sled team has been because of the attentiveness of Murphy's Law. He expressed to the media that what is meant is *"whatever could go wrong, will go wrong."*

Universal Truths

Even though this law catches the world-weary, negative view of the world, it does not stand alone. Sharp spectators have now come up with a few of their laws later its fame after the rocket sled trials at Edwards Air Force Base.

A few have become sought-after in their right. One example of this is the *Peter Principle*, telling that every individual will be supported by his or her degree of ineffectiveness. You will find hundreds of rules, observations, and principles, which have been made after Murphy's Law. A few of them are strange, some are funny, and some are wise.

The Appeal and the Fatalism of Murphy's Law

What makes Murphy's Law a universal principle? In spite of everything, you have a 50% chance of getting things right when approaching an electrical socket along with a 2-divided plug engineered to fit one way only. You also have a 50% chance of getting things wrong, as well. Maybe, the perfect clarification to this is the underlying sense of fatalism.

In case you didn't know yet, fatalism is the concept telling everyone is defenseless to the urges of fate. That type of perspective tells that the things, which occur to every person, are inevitable. It is the concept that there is universal law at work, which takes a delight at playing with you.

However, fatalism opposes another principle – free will. That is the concept that human beings acquire the free will and that every choice, together with the effects that come with those options is your own.

Probably, our link to this law is the outcome of the collision among fatalism and free will. Meanwhile, Murphy's Law shows us our own irrefutable foolishness. If allowed to do something not right, we will do so around half of the time. However, that depends on our own options. This law also showcases how they are lacking in control.

Murphy's Law does not ascertain anything. It does not even discuss anything. It only tells a saying: *things will go wrong.* Nonetheless, we fail to recall that there are other powers at work when you contemplate this law. Rudyard Kipling said that how many instances you drop a piece of bread, it will always land on the ground butter-side down. Recognized as the author of *The Jungle Book,* Kipling was made an observation, which many people can always relate to – life is complicated, almost to a ridiculous level.

Talking about the buttered piece of bread, you must remember the reality that one side is always heavier than the other. That denotes that on its way to the earth, the weighty part will flip to the surface because of gravity. However, it won't flip through around back to the top for a similar reason. Consequently, it's weightier than the part without the butter. That makes Kipling correct. A slice of buttered bread will land butter-side down.

Always take note that Murphy's Law is all about life. It talks about the significance of forward-thinking and changing your point of view about the negative scenarios life throws you away repeatedly.

From another view, Murphy's Law refers to recognizing the opportunities. The seeds inside each problem must grow into affirmative results whenever you take a new test. Ultimately, Murphy's Law is all about YOU. This tackles how you approach life and converting your "lemons" into a fresh bottle of lemonade. It will always be up to you if you can work it or not.

Chapter 6

Occam's Razor

The simplest explanation is normally the correct one. You have probably heard this statement before. Detectives utilize it to assume who is the possible suspect in a murder case. Also, doctors utilize it to identify the illness behind a collection of symptoms.

That line of reason is known as the *Occam's razor.* It is utilized in a broad spectrum of ways around the globe as a way to divide a situation or a concern and to remove unnecessary elements. However, what we refer as the razor is a bit different from what its author penned.

You will find two different parts, which are known the basis of Occam's razor:

1. **The Principle of Parsimony** – It's impractical to do along with more what's finished with less.
2. **The Principle of Plurality** – It must not be postulated without necessity.

They symbolize the foundation of the study of humankind into the universe. It also represents the way you perceive your surroundings. There is no telling which type of world you would reside in now without Occam's razor.

You can consider basic systems found in nature, such as plants and viruses and their capability to perform complicated task like photosynthesis and infection. People put importance to such basic models. When we talk about fabricated structures, people are more likely to source structures on what they previously know. All of that points to the philosophies of parsimony and plurality.

One crucial aspect this law shows is the subjectivity of how you perceive the world. Indeed, the sky is blue. You are aware by that through starting at it. Nonetheless, what shadow of blue is it?

The Origin of Occam's Razor

You might be thinking that Occam is the name of a person. It's not. Occam is a town located in England where William of Occam was born. He lived in the middle of 1285 to 1349, through the medieval period. It's the era where surnames were not typical, and citizens were recognized by their place of origin.

William lived as a Franciscan monk and a philosopher. He was a pious person who took his vow of poverty. That means he lived only what's needed. The foundation of the Occam's razor was a well-established line of medieval ideas by the time of William. He obtained the essence of the law and packed it in a manner, which can be easily comprehended. He was able to encapsulate a world of medieval logic through making a couple of easy sentences. He guarantees its safe way into the modern period.

How Does Occam's Razor Work?

You are already aware that Occam's razor is the principle of simplicity or parsimony following the basic theory tends to be real. Occam didn't formulate this principle. It is invented by Aristotle, Aquinas and other great philosophers Occam read. Even though Occam didn't make a debate for the validity of the principle, he was able to utilize it in different ways. That's the main reason why it's connected with him.

For a few, the principle of simplicity tells the world is simple. For instance, Aquinas debates that nature doesn't use two mechanisms where one serves. That understanding is also proposed by its most famous construction: *entities must not be multiplied beyond necessity.*

However, that's a problematic assertion. Today, you know that nature is terminated in both function and form. Even though medieval thinkers were hugely oblivious of evolional biology, they support the occurrence of a supreme God. In any case, Occam never makes that kind of supposition, and he doesn't utilize famous construction of the belief.

For him, the law of simplicity obstructs the development of hypotheses, not certain individuals. Occam thinks that theories aren't intended to perform things such as predicting and explaining. Those things could be obtained more efficiently with fewer expectations.

For a few, it might be a common sense. Presume your vehicle stops working and your fuel gauge tells an empty gas tank. It would be funny to assume both that you're out of gas and oil. You just need one hypothesis to explain what has taken place.

Others would object that the law of simplicity can't assure the truth. Even though the razor looks like a common sense, when utilized in science, it could strong and amazing impacts.

Who Utilizes Occam's Razor?

Scientists are the people who utilize Occam's razor the most. Scientist utilizes the law to get from one pint to another in a specific data set to make their way through huge equations.

Some skeptics also utilize the principle as a vital device and as evidence. In case you didn't know yet, skeptics are individuals who are more likely to believe what they could sense. That makes them foils to individuals who have faith in religious beliefs and conspiracy theories.

However, a real skeptic will explain to you that he only utilizes the principle as a tool for consideration various justifications. Skeptics who value the healthy examination of the universe utilize Occam's razor to have the easiest clarification. Nonetheless, they fall short of utilizing it to discount other, more complicated reasons.

But some scientists and skeptics wield the razor similar to a broadsword. To those individuals, it verifies one theory and contradicts to others. You will find two different issues when you are utilizing Occam's razor as a device to disprove or prove an explanation. First, it can identify whether or not something is subjective. It means it depends on the person to interpret its simplicity. Second, there is no proof, which backs the notion that simplicity is equivalent to truth.

It's essential to bear in mind that the concept credited to Aristotle says that perfection is seen in simplicity is a fabricated concept. It is not supported by physics, chemistry, or math. Nevertheless, it is taken by other people as truthful.

You will find a few creationists who will claim that Occam's razor shows their ideology is right. Consequently, its easy explanation to tell that God created everything in the universe. That's far better than telling it was formed by a Big Bang that was followed by different interconnected accidents.

Another example is the evolutionist. That clarification that God is present, but we have no proof that he truly does. That's the same case for atheists who do not believe in God. These people utilize Occam's razor together with the concept of Aristotle of simplicity corresponding perfection to claim there's no God.

The only issue with such arguments is that what establishes simplicity is subjective. Aside from that, you can't prove that the universe could be any basic.

At this point, you must have enough idea of how Occam's razor is utilized to improve one idea over the other.

Chapter 7: Hanlon's Razor

Have you ever sensed that the universe is all against you? If so, we want you to know that you aren't alone. Everyone has a tendency to think that when something goes wrong, the fault lies in some conspiracy against you.

For instance, your officemate fails to present you a report on time. They ought to be attempting to ruin your job and beat you to a promotion. Your kid falls and ruins a costly plate. They ought to be attempting to annoy you and waste your precious time.

However, the truth is that such explanations you likely to jump are infrequently true. Perhaps you officemate thought today was Thursday, not Friday. Perhaps your kid has sticky hands from playing. You see, that's where Hanlon's razor enters.

What is Hanlon's Razor?

Hanlon's Razor is a very practical mental model. Similar to Occam's razor, it's a vital tool for quick, intelligent cognition and decision-making.

Using Hanlon's razor enables us to establish relationships better. It also enables you to become less judgmental, and it enhances your nationality. It allows you to offer individuals the gain of the doubt and have more empathy. That way, the importance of Hanlon's razor is pronounced in business and relationships matter.

It's widely known that most people spend most of the day communicating with other people. They also make choices according to those. You lead complicated lives wherein things are continuously going wrong *(as what Murphy's law tells)*. When that takes place, a typical feedback is to a fault to the closest person and thinks they have malevolent intent.

Human beings are fast to accuse politicians, companies, their managers, employees, etc. trying to derail them. You overlook how many times you have jostled someone in the street or overlooked to meet your friend on time. As an alternative, the culprit becomes the source of intense annoyance.

To think intent in such a scenario tends to worsen the issue. None of you could ever determine what somebody else wanted to take place. The most intelligent person makes numerous mistakes. Negligence or inability is far likely to be the source than cruelty.

When a scenario causes you to become exasperated o irritated, it could be appreciated to consider when such emotions are acceptable. Sometimes, the ideal way to react to other individuals causing you some problem is by informing them and not to contempt them. With that, you can prevent a repetition of the same scenario.

The Origins of Hanlon's Razor

The words *Hanlon's razor* was invented, Robert J. Hanlon. However, it has been voiced by various individuals throughout history since 1774.

The Advantages of Employing Hanlon's razor

You might find that Hanlon's razor might be advantageous for two different reasons:

1. **It is recommended for you to begin thinking for another reason than malice for negative situations**

   Generally, considering malice as a source of a negative situation will only cause you to feel more stress and anger than thinking of other reasons. Thus, you could benefit from not thinking the worst from the beginning. That's true, especially when it comes to your emotional productivity and emotional wellbeing.

2. **Hanlon's razor could help you see the most logical explanation for different events**

   It is more likely that individuals will do something that is out of their lack of mindfulness than out of a planned desire to cause any danger.

Employing Hanlon's razor could help you evaluate faster the scenarios that you're currently in. It could help you handle those cases in a much better way.

From a philosophical point of view, using this principle could be perceived as *"doing the right thing."* That's because it shares the principle of charity. It represents the concept that you must begin by thinking about the best possible understanding of other people's actions and speeches.

Using that standpoint is also advantageous for non-philosophical motives. Offering individuals the gain of the doubt at first could help you interact with productively. That also makes them cooperate with you more in the end. That's vital in relationships, both professional and personal. This is where thinking that the other individual did something that had undesirable result out of hatred could be harmful if you end up being mistaken.

Hanlon's razor enables you to be ready to take the necessary action that you otherwise would not. For instance, think of a situation where somebody is doing something, which troubles you so much. That could be a scenario where your next-door neighbor is making too much noise. Unconsciously, you might begin to think that they're conscious of what they're doing is troubling you but they do not care. That is the type of mindset, which causes you to think that you must not care to ask them to stop.

Nonetheless, using Hanlon's razor could help you think they're doing it not because they do not put their attention about troubling you. They are not just not aware that what they are doing is troubling you. That could support you to take some good action. For instance, you might ask them to stop that might not have done otherwise.

Employing Hanlon's razor provides different advantages. That includes assisting you to feel less worried. It also helps you interact better with other people. Later on, you will notice how you could use Hanlon's razor to gain from it.

How to Use Hanlon's razor

Hanlon's razor could be used whenever you have time to seek a reason for why somebody has done something, which ended up having negative effects. You will notice particular guidelines, which will help you use Hanlon's razor efficiently. It could be by extending its scope, by understanding how to evaluate the scenario or by accounting for the egocentric bias.

Exemptions to Hanlon's razor

Hanlon's razor is considered a criterion. However, it must be perceived as a guiding principle instead of an absolute truth. You will find some cases where a negative result must be credited to malice instead of obliviousness and foolishness.

That denotes, although you must aim to offer individuals the gain of the doubt where possible, using Hanlon's razor should not cause you to be not prepared and immature. Therefore, every time you are planning to use Hanlon's razor, you must consider the following aspects:

- **What are the costs linked with *improperly* assuming reasons aside from malice?**

  The pricier it would be for you to think wrongly that somebody acted for a reason aside from malice, the more careful you must be when using this principle.

- **What are the possible costs connected with improperly supposing malice?**

  The pricier it would be for you to assume malice improperly, the more inclined you must be to think that whatever occurred had taken place because of a motive aside from malice.

- **How likely it is that an action took place because of reasons aside from malice?**

   The more probable it is that what occurred did not happen because of malice, the more inclined you must be to presenting the other individual the gain of the doubt. Every time you evaluate that probability, you could consider the past actions of the individual. You can also consider their skills, their general personality, and what they stand to gain from acting malevolently.

You will also find other cases where you might prefer not to employ Hanlon's razor. That's because the probability of the other individual acting malevolently is high. Maybe there's a high price to improperly thinking that their actions didn't happen because of malice.

On those situations, it could be advantageous to begin by thinking malice. Then take a different explanation after you have enough proof telling otherwise.

Always remember that those scenarios could be designated using the idea of *"guilty until proven innocent."* That's the opposite of the idea presented by Hanlon's razor, describing *"innocent until proven guilty."*

Always remember that it could be advantageous to utilize a hybrid strategy. For instance, that could involve thinking non-malicious clarification for other's action and getting ready to act when the hateful explanation becomes true.

Chapter 8: Pareto Principle

The Pareto principle is the adage wherein 80 percent of the results are driven from 20 percent of causes. For instance, whenever you are watching movies. It could mean that 20 percent of the movies, which are being presented, in theaters is accountable for 80 percent of ticket sales.

The 'results' and 'causes' that the principle talks about are varied in nature. It depends on the situation at hand. Another example, 'results' could talk about anything from consumer complaints, financial revenue to acquisition knowledge. However, the 'causes' could mean anything from time spent working, to the features of the software and financial investment.

The Pareto principle has been used in different scenarios. In fact, it has predictive value when we talk about individuals and big groups. Because it's simple to implement and very efficient, it can be useful to know how it works.

A Few Samples of the Pareto Principle

One of the most sought-after examples of this principle is connected to Vilfredo Pareto. He was an economist in Italy, which this principle is coined. Vilfredo noticed that 80 percent of the prosperity in his country is acquired by 20 percent of the population.

You will also find other scenarios where the Pareto principle could be applied. Some of these are the following:

1. A research on software engineering discovered that at least 20 percent of the modules cause 80 percent of its operational errors.

2. A research that assessed flow patterns in libraries discovered that at least 20 percent of the books in the library account for 80 percent of its flow.

3. A research that assessed shopping trends at convenient stores discovered that at least 20 percent of the consumers account for 80 percent of the sales of the store.

The Scientific Foundation for the Pareto Principle

You need to bear in mind that the Pareto principle is sourced on the idea of *power laws.* In short, a power law is a kind of functional connection concerning two quantities. A linear transformation in one quantity results to exponential transformation in the other quantity. That means one quantity differs in proportion along with the power of the other.

The Pareto principle recommends that in most scenarios, you could anticipate noticing a Pareto distribution. That's a particular kind of power-law distribution having a negative exponent. That denotes one quantity grows, the other quantity lowers as a power of initial quantity.

For instance, a distribution of Pareto could take place in the connection between several earners and income level. When you raise the income level by three, you can get nine times fewer people to gain that much.

As a particular outcome level raises, the ration of causes accountable for it reduces. That principle applies to a different real-world variable.

Caution about 20/80 Distributions

You might be aware already that the Pareto principle talks about a particular kind of Pareto distribution. The 80 percent of results come from 20 percent of the causes. Nonetheless, the distribution is not limited to an 80-20 division. Often, you will find a variability about the strict distributions that are seen.

For instance, the distribution may include an 85-15 split, 75-25 split, and so much more. For that reason, the specific distribution won't matter anymore. That's true, particularly when you use the Pareto principle. You need to bear in mind that a small quantity of the causes will be accountable for a big part of the results.

How to Use the Pareto Principle

The objective of this law is to help you focus your efforts effectively. It enables you to concentrate on the small number of causes accountable for a big amount of outcomes. That denotes you must concentrate on the 20 percent of the work, leading to 80 percent of the positive results.

An example of this would be the following:

- Are you designing a software product? You must concentrate on the 20 percent of the features, which are vital to the 80 percent of the users.

- Are you studying for your test? You must concentrate on the 20 percent of the material that accounts for 80 percent of the questions.
- Are you operating a commercial business? You must concentrate on working along with the 20 percent of the consumers who produce 80 percent of your revenue.

What's more, it also denotes you must seek a way on how you can deal with it or remove the 20 percent problems accountable for eighty percent of your negative results. A good example of this would be the following:

- Prevent the 20 percent of the physical exercises that cause 80 percent of the accidents.
- Resolve the 20 percent of the bugs that result in 80 percent of the reports.
- Stay away from working the 20 percent of the customers who generate 80 percent of the criticisms.

Always take note that there could be an overlap between the causes, which result in the positive results and the ones, which result in the negative results. Now, what can you do when this takes place? What will you do when 20 percent of the material you need to study will account for 80 percent of the questionnaires on the test? You must take time to comprehend the material even when that causes eighty percent of your problems.

Nevertheless, you will find some cases where the optimal course of action is not that obvious. For instance, when 20 percent of the consumers produce 80 percent of your income, but also 80 percent of the criticisms. When this takes place, you need to take into account your priorities before you decide the best action.

Guidelines When Using the Pareto Principle

In this section, we will provide you some tips you need to bear in mind when using the Pareto principle:

1. **The Pareto principle is not all about the 80-20 distribution.**

   Even though the principle refers to the 80-20 distribution, you might also encounter different types of distributions. It could be 70-30 or 90-10. Seeking for scenarios where a trivial quantity of causes is accountable for a big ratio of results is important. That's the best thing to do instead of seeking a particular proportion between results and causes.

2. **The Pareto principle does not apply in all scenarios.**

   You won't find assurance that it will also apply in the circumstance you're dealing with today, even though most usual scenarios present a Pareto distribution. Further, you will find other cases where another distribution might be more valuable.

3. There tends to be substantial variation even with the top 20 percent and the bottom 80 percent.

You might notice a huge variation even with people who belong to every group. When your sample is big enough, you might notice that the top 20 percent and bottom 80 percent bottom could be divided using an 80-20 distribution.

For instance, 20 percent of earners within the population. You will find a massive variation amid the upper few individuals who gain the most, and the rest of the crowd.

Are you dealing with a continuing process? Then it's vital that you re-assess your situation every now and then. You could amend after based on the Pareto principle every time. That's because the distribution between the applicable results and causes might change in the long run.

Ultimately, when you apply the Pareto principle, you must ensure to employ common sense. Always consider the further factors, which might be vital beyond the cause-result link. For instance, you are trying to launch a software service. However, you are trying to choose which bugs to resolve according to the number of users who reported them. It's more likely that you like to fix a bug, which could cause crucial security problems, even when one user only noticed it.

Chapter 9: Sturgeon's Law

"90% of all things are crap." That saying is what Sturgeon's law represents. It indicates the belief that most work that is generated in any field is poor quality. For instance, books, the law tells that ninety percent of the books, which come out yearly are comparatively poor.

That idea is an advantageous criterion. Bearing this in mind could help enhance how a person evaluates and use information. It also helps in the way in which a person chooses which tasks to work on.

The Origins of the Sturgeon's Law

Did you know that Sturgeon's Law was initially referred to as the *Sturgeon's revelation?* It was proposed in 1950 by the American author Theodore Sturgeon as part of his cover of the value of science fiction books being printed.

The law was initially mentioned around 1951 in New York University. Later on, it was popularized at the World-Con Science-fiction convention in 1953.

The goal of this law is to point out that even most science fiction writing is poor, that should not be employed to attack science fiction as a genre. That's because most products and works in any type of sectors are poor as well.

For that reason, Sturgeon announced that science-fiction writing is not different from other types of writing. It's true irrespective of the reality that critics condemned it more severely.

Real-Life Examples of the Sturgeon's Law

You will find different instances of this law in different fields. Some of these are the following:

- Most new products launched today are of poor quality. That denotes they are not worth buying.
- Most new television shows today are of poor quality. They are not worth viewing.
- Most new books launched in the bookstores today are poor quality. That means they aren't worth reading anymore.

Indeed, Sturgeon's law thinks that ninety percent of all things are crap. It is hard to enumerate the exact number of works that are of poor quality. In the majority of cases, it's hard to identify what contributes to poor quality and what does not.

That kind of problem is predominant in situations where the supposed quality of a specific work varies on the standpoint of the person evaluating it. For instance, there are some books, which some individuals will consider as excellent while some will consider they are awful. That's because the last group is composed of individuals who are not attracted to the subject the books cover.

That's vital to bear in mind considering the applications of the Sturgeon's law. In most cases, the classification of what's good and what's not is random. It will still vary on the personal preference of the person.

How Can You Use the Sturgeon's Law?

Below are some guidelines you can follow when you decided to apply Sturgeon's law:

- **As a Creator**

    It could be advantageous to apply this law if you are somebody who makes products or content. The principle could guide you determine what type of things to concentrate on within your work.

You can start by evaluating the existing market. Notice how your work ranks compared to current products. Identify whether or not what you're making is value your time. Mostly, unless you could design work, which is in the top ten percent, there's no point to reproducing it. You will only be backing to the noise. You can simply add to the lower ninety percent of works, which the majority of individuals disregard.

One way you could gain as a creator is that it a small minority of the work that you generate will have to huge effect. But that's alright. Knowing the Sturgeon's law could be advantageous whenever you are learning; helping you set your own realistic goals.

As a creator, you should concentrate on making something, which is unique, given that the products available today are of poor quality. Stop producing something, which contributes to the noise. Concentrate on showing only your greatest work unless you are creating something as part of your learning skill.

- **As a critic**

  The principle could be advantageous if you are playing the role of a critic. That's because it could help you think not to waste your time disapproving defective things. After all, those things must not be taken seriously.

  Using Sturgeon's law as a critic could be relevant when evaluating things fairly. That's because a big amount of the works given in a field tend to be low quality irrespective of what the field is. Therefore, you must not judge a field because it has subpar works. You must not concentrate on the weaker aspects of something every time you are condemning it.

  Based on Sturgeon's law, it could be seen as an extension of the principle of charity. That simply entails that you must concentrate on the stronger features of a claim when condemning it.

You see, it might be simple to concentrate on the inferior features of something when condemning it. However, it will only be a waste of time, leading unlikely to a productive conversation. Thus, you must try to concentrate on stronger elements of whatever it is you're condemning instead of its weaker aspects.

- **As a consumer**

Sturgeon's law is also advantageous for a consumer. It helps you become a more practical person regarding how you use your money, effort, and time. That's true, especially when buying items or consuming information.

One way you can use Sturgeon's law as a consumer is to think of your decision about which product to purchase or which content to consume as a *zero-sum game.* That is where the resources you give to something of inferior quality could instead be devoted to something more valuable.

That denotes each time you waste loading your mind with poor information is a time you could spend on something worthy. Poor and subpar information will only take up significant mental space in the end. That could even lead to transferring high quality material.

You will see different methods that you utilize in an attempt to prevent the low quality of ninety percent of the material out there. For instance, you must check the reviews first before you purchase a book. That will help you decide if it fits your interest and it helps you to know if people trust it's worth reading.

The majority of what is out there is of low quality, whether when it comes to apps, articles, movies, books, and so much more. Do not waste your money and time on those low-quality items. As an alternative, understand how to determine the high-quality stuff, and concentrate on them.

Basic Guidelines

Sturgeon's law must be used along with common sense. Acknowledge the fact that Sturgeon is a practical rule of thumb. It must be valued as such instead of absolute truth.

Often, the ratio of works that's worth of your time might be ten percent. However, sometimes that will end up being the same but different figures, like twenty percent or five percent. Concentrate on the underlying idea behind it rather than trying to quantify the law with exact metrics.

The best works in a particular sector are not randomly distributed among various creators. When we talk about literature, when ten percent of new literature books are worth reading, a substantial portion of them may be written by similar authors.

You could expect ten percent of the works to be of good quality. Nonetheless, only a small amount out of that ten percent will be of great quality. The more time you could concentrate on the great works, the less you'll waste time on unnecessary stuff.

Always ensure that are you not blindly adopting it as a guard for a particular area. Sturgeon's law could be valuable in a few scenarios. However, always mention it in a manner, which explains what makes it valuable. That will prevent depending on misleading reasoning.

Chapter 10: Parkinson's Law

"The work multiplies to fill the time that is accessible for its accomplishment." That is the adage of the Parkinson's Law, indicating that the more time you consume to a particular activity, the longer it will take to finish it. That's true even if you could've gotten the activity finished in a shorter time.

If you have one week to do a task, which could take you a day to finish, you'll end up extending your performance of that activity, until it brings you a week to finish it. This law has vital effects in different situations. It could have an impact on boosting your own productivity and predicting other individual's behavior.

What is included in Parkinson's Law?

The occurrence described by this law has been perceived in different scientific research. It tells that when individuals are given further time to finish a certain task, they'll take advantage of it, although they don't need it really. That doesn't result in an improved presentation on the job.

What's more, that implication often extends to further attempts to do a similar activity. When somebody is allowed further time to do a task the first time, it'll take slower than needed to finish the task in the end.

What this research tells is when individuals are given an activity to do, they think of "*how much time do I need to finish it?*" They do not consider how much time they need to finish it. That type of standpoint causes individuals to waste their time by working inefficiently.

Real Life Examples of Parkinson's Law

No matter if you're aware of it or not, you have already encountered Parkinson's law many times in your life. Below are some real life examples of this principle:

1. All year you are aware that you had a beach vacation or wedding vacation to get prepared. However, you put off healthy eating and exercise and went on a crash diet 4 weeks before your travel.

2. You had all week to finish the proposal, but you waited to finish it until 5:30 PM on Friday.

3. You had all whole semester to write your paper. However, you wrote it within the last 48 hours before the deadline. You sent it in at 4 AM in the morning it was due.

Have you experienced any of those situations? If so, you are aware of what we are talking about here. For weeks or months on end, you are paralyzed and not capable of working. Then, you suddenly become a engine during the last week before a job has to be completed.

The Origins of Parkinson's Law

Cyril Parkinson is a British historian who observed the trend through his time, along with the British Civil Service. Cyril explained that as bureaucracies lengthened, they became more incompetent and unproductive. He also applied this reflection to different other scenarios. They realize that as the size of something raised, its effectiveness lowered.

Cyril discovered that even a collection of easy activities raised in difficulty to load the time assigned to it. The job becomes easier and simpler to fix as the length of time assigned to an activity became shorter.

The principle goes hand in hand with the conviction that you need to work very hard. That kind of thinking is mirrored in the fact that managers often reward employees for hours instead of hours spent working or outcomes generated.

Parkinson's Law as a Productivity Tool

How can you take advantage of Parkinson's Law in your own work? Begin every job by determining its scope. You could try to identify how much time it will take to finish it.

Don't ask how much time you need to finish the job. As an alternative, ask yourself how much time it must take you to finish that job. Do all your best to finish the work in that given timeframe.

But how can you achieve it? You can achieve that by employing simulated time restraints. The study tells that it could result in higher outputs. Every restraint will apply to a particular job. For instance, you might utilize a timer for those short-term activities. You might prefer to use a date-based deadline for those long-term activities.

It's okay if you result in noticing that more time is needed. Nevertheless, try to finish the job before the allocated time runs out. Make sure you do it without compromising the worth of the effort. When you do this, you guarantee you don't fall into the trap of using the added time you have even if you don't really need it at all. In case you require less time than you initially thought, you can try to complete the job ahead of time. Do not allow it to drag you on.

More Uses of Parkinson's Law

The scenarios you noticed so far are emphasized under the framework of how much time you must use on chores. However, the same deliberations apply to other resources like effort and money. That denotes you must not pour resources into particular activity only because they are accessible.

Do you want to prevent this downside? Ask yourself first what advantageous results you could assume to get for the assets you wish to invest. Ensure the proportion between results-gained to resources-utilized is sufficient.

Are you thinking how much time you must spend on a particular activity? Your objective is to understand what resources you need to finish the task. Ask yourself that question instead of taking advantage of the resources you have, even if they're not needed.

Take note that Parkinson's Law helps you engage more efficiently along with other individuals. You can employ the strategies you read here to set goals and restrictions in cooperative work. Make sure that the flow of your work is as effective as possible.

What You Need to Remember

There's an important thing you need to take note of Parkinson's law. When selecting how much time or resources to dedicate to a job, pick an amount that ensures you do not waste anything unnecessarily. Make sure you also do not compromise the value of your effort.

Concentrate on setting realistic time constraints when accounting this principle. Ensure you follow by them as much as possible. That's as opposed to performing stuff like setting fewer time constraints that will ensure you don't spend excessive time on every job, leading to inferior work.

For instance, you are aware that a particular task takes at least ten minutes to finish. Knowing that will allow you to finish the task within two minutes without cramming and still do a wonderful job. Your aim here must be to determine that it takes at least ten minutes to finish the job. You need to set that time as your time limit, avoiding yourself by wasting thirty minutes on it only because you can.

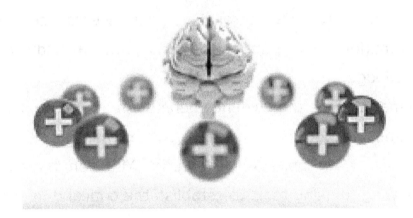

Chapter 11: Useful Thinking Tools

Critical thinking is a vital ability, which moves a person from concrete ideas to abstract and conditional ideas. Critical thinking enables you to assess results, compare insights, determine parallels, order events, create information, and pull conclusions from a body of knowledge.

No matter if it's the evidence behind a math formula or an implied tone in your essay, critical thinking allows you to solve topics in real-world. You can try the following thinking tools to establish the critical thinking skills needed for success.

1. Mind Mapping

   Did you know that mind mapping is considered the small black dress of idea generation? It doesn't lose its style. In fact, it would feel wrong to walk into a company and not notice some type of mind map on a whiteboard anywhere.

The key to mind mapping is to remember each idea, which comes up. Do not ignore anything; however far-fetch it might look. You must save all the crucial selection procedure later on. Produce as many ideas as possible. Simply put, the more ideas you write, the higher the chance of getting that golden ticket idea.

2. Get up and Get Out

Individuals often undervalue the worth of being bored. When you work around the screens throughout the day, it could prove both pleasing and comforting to get up and walk for a bit. You must allow your mind to roam around rather than concentrating on a task so difficult, it hurts you. Why don't you walk around your local woods? Pamper yourself in your own personal contemplation montage as you skin stuns across a phone. Allow the magic of nature and the short moment of what is hopefully serene and peace, motivate and invigorate you.

A lot of people think that the practice of meditation is a wonderful way to help initiate creativity. Allow yourself to be a deep peace. You will notice how individuals might find it very soothing.

3. Adjust your Point of View

It could be difficult to achieve. However, try to position yourself in other's shoes. Often, you could be too connected to your work. Yes, and we always do it. You might be too close to see some errors that are evident from afar.

You can start sharing your ideas along with other people. Get a new pair of eyes to check at your work. Start to support constructive criticism. There's no need for you to take it all on board. It might provide up practical and helpful observations.

4. Picture Association

Are you stuck for any ideas? You can do an image search on your subject of choice. Select a random image. Work backward from the image, and you will create a story around how the image was taken.

For instance, you notice an image of a cat gazing up at the night sky. You can ask yourself what the cat could be thinking it its mind. Is it a stargazing cat? Does that cat furtively long to be an astronomer? Maybe a story about a space cat would be amazing. A space cat would make a wonderful mascot for any business.

5. Random Word Generation

This thinking tool is very simple. You only need to choose two random words and try to connect your content to it imaginatively. Basic as that.

The fun part here is how you pick to come up with the phrases and words. You could utilize an online generator tool. You can riffle through a dictionary, or you could write some words on some plastic balls. Then select the words on the first two balls you catch.

6. Lateral Thinking

This thinking tool is invented by Dr. de Bono that involves thinking in your scenario differently. The easiest answer isn't always correct. You resolve the majority of the problems in a linear way. For example, when something takes place, it should have… because of…

You take the step-by-step method of seeking your answers. Dr. de Bono supports other individuals to view their situation differently. Step sideways for a moment if you would. Doing this enables you to re-assess your predicament from a more creative standpoint.

For instance, you have customers who sell tractors. Are you thinking, linearly? If so, you might feel the necessity to write content about how excellent tractors are, as you need to sell tractors. Thinking about stuff, laterally opens up a new world of possibilities. You must try to look at the big picture.

What's more, tractors are a vital component to resources; farming produces food and farming as general. Take note that farms are house animals as well. A sought-after children's rhyme about farm animals is the Old McDonald. You might think about how that rhyme came to be. Why don't you make content around the origin of that rhyme?

That's only a basic instance. However, you could notice how lateral thinking could be utilized to help motivate you.

7. Six Thinking Hats

This thinking tool is also invented by Dr. Edward de Bono during the early eighties. This famous method is now utilized by different businesses across the globe. It involves putting on a collection of metaphorical hats when making a decision. Always remember that every hat symbolizes a new direction of thinking:

- o Bluet Hat – Control
- o Green Hat – Creativity
- o Yellow Hat – Logic
- o Black Hat – Caution and Judgment
- o Red Hat – Emotions
- o White Hat – Facts

This thinking tool could be utilized on your own or in a group. You might find yourself wearing more than one hat. You could utilize the hats to take the ego out of the balance. They allow you to think and choose topics in a rational yet creative manner.

8. The Checklist

Young kids are extremely imaginative. Their craving, creativity, and curiosity for knowledge appear to be limitless. They always ask questions about all things on the planet. But why? That's because everything is new to their eyes.

Have you ever tried to play the *"Why"* game along with a child? If yes, you will understand what we're trying to say here. It is annoying yet amazingly informative.

Now, as you get older, you are more likely to stop asking too many questions. You accept more, as it has been explained to you before. Perhaps that's the reason why most adults are viewed as having very less imagination by younger generations.

Alex Osborn is the man who is often referred to as the father of brainstorming. He developed around seventy-five creative questions to help support ideas in his book, *"Applied Imagination."* This book is worth a read once you are acquainted of it. However, to present to you some ideas, you will find universal questions, which could be asked:

- How?
- What?
- Who?
- When?
- Where?
- Why?

You can ask these questions to yourself each time you make some content. The probabilities are you will come up with some interesting answers.

Chapter 12: Creative Problem Solving

Creative Problem Solving is one of those key idea generation methods. Today, it's not sufficient on its own, although better service quality is vital. Without creativity and innovation, you can't expect to accomplish long-term success at a global level.

What is Creative Problem Solving?

CPS might be described as a problem solving method, which addresses a problem creatively. The key is creative as it's not apparent. The answer must solve the confirmed issue originally with the answer being grasped freely.

In the 1950s, Alex Osborn and Dr. Sidney J. Parnes invented the Osborn-Parnes (CPS) processes of solving problems creatively. The difference between this method and several Creative Problem Solving methods is that there the usage of both divergent and convergent for thinking within the sequence of every process step.

Every stage begins with a divergent thinking. It's a broad hunt for various options. After that come convergent thinking, involving assessing and choosing.
Different Models of Creative Problem Solving

You can think of no less than 4 models when defining the Osborn-Parness process of CPS:

1. Systematic

The Thinking Skills Model is a type of system along with different entry points identified by the task or scenario. The structure in this model is a contract along with your present web-like unified perception of the universe.

It portrays the unique core of every phase of renaming. This model informs you what takes place. You might observe that the diamonds sustain. What's more, the three-core focus point unites in solid colors along with the starting point varying along with the situational prerequisite.

2. Bubble

During the 1990s, the diamond figures transformed into attached bubbles. It represents behavior shifts towards meaningful and directed connectedness. Directed freedom gests broader birth. You will find three distinct phrases in the bubble model.

This tells approval to go in not just at the initial stage, but at any stage of the procedure. The linear model features diamond shapes along with flawless edges. You will also find arrows to offer directions. The 3 bubbles in this model allow you to understand what you must do exactly.

3. Linear

In this model, each of the six phases of the CPS process is defined by a diamond shape. That shape represents diverging, generating, and first options. Then, it will be followed by a set of a refreshed focus and moving on.

Models & Stages of CPS

You will find six different levels in the Osborne-Parnes process of CPS.

- **Objective Finding**

  Identifying the goal of defining your favored output is the foundation of the CPS strategy. Often, individuals pay no attention to particular aspects of the issue, initiating the obscurement of the thought process. The individual fails to consider the big picture. Defining the objective offers a lucid concept about the issue, which facilitates the study of different potential solutions to it.

- **Fact Finding**

  Gathering information about the issue and linked data is vital for understanding the problem. You can start creating a list of core information like who and what's involved, your perceptions and assumptions, standpoints of interested parties, facts, and feelings. These might help you start the process of constructing ideas.

- **Problem Finding**

Identify potential challenges which might come about and the potential opportunities present inside of it. You can do that by utilizing the problem objective as well as the collected data. That would help you with focusing on the issue. It's very easy to shift your attention away from the goal and to have the answers to the wrong problems.

- **Idea Finding**

Recycling an answer when you encounter a problem you potentially experienced beforehand is a simple procedure. Your mind senses 'conceptual blocks' which is composed of challenges like faithfulness, solidity, satisfaction, and promise. Such obstruct you from thinking creatively and creating new ideas. Therefore, you must brainstorm and identify as many potential solutions as you could.

- **Solution Finding**

  What is next after you have done with having new concepts? The next thing you need to do is to evaluate them to know if they meet your requirement for success and to know if it could be implemented. You can improvise, reinforce, and choose the ideal concept. Ensure that the solutions aren't just an innovative but helpful tool. Sometimes, determination is the key solution.

- **Acceptance Finding**

  You've picked the best potential resolution, which is functional and pleases the prerequisites for success. What you need to do now is to determine your roles. Identify the best steps to use the accessible resources.

How to Use CPS in a Business Setting

Whatever the issue or need your business might be dealing with, fresh approaches and creative ideas could make the difference. It provides a way to introduce change into an organization, which lowers the normal fear, which accompanies change. What's more, the process of creative problem solving turns out to be a change agent. It could convert resistance into action.

Perceiving a Problem as a Chance

One of the vital features of the CPS process is that it converts a problem into a change to enhance the company. The creative approach supports individuals to participate in a dynamic environment that supports new approaches and ideas. You can do that rather than depending on conventional ideas or past practices to fix a problem.

The reality is that the majority of organizations have the creative ability in their own environment among the staff. That creative procedure brings together different individuals. It includes line workers, office personnel, managers, supervisors, and so much more. The individuals selected to participate varies on the problem being fixed.

The creative procedure also follows a format that brings the group up to the time when creative thinking is uncovered. In the preliminary stages, the procedure achieves the following:

- Concentrates on how to sell the creative concept
- Establishes criteria for selecting ideas
- Supports participants
- Develops goals
- Determines the problem traditionally

Famous creative problem solving methods that have been established include mind mapping, brainstorming, or team game playing. The aim is to nurture individuals to feel at ease to generate ideas freely without the anxiety of disapprovals.

The Path of Creativity

In both mind mapping and brainstorming, concepts are recommended that may or may not appear sensible on the surface. However, no concept is removed, and every idea is acknowledged. One concept is associated with or mapped with other ideas. Path of ideas results to one or more creative solutions to a concern. The solution picked varies on the criteria developed at the start of the procedure.

In CPS, members of the organization are supported to join. The procedure offers acknowledgment to the individuals who are the main contributors to the success of the business. It supports positive energy, creative approaches, collaboration, as well as teamwork. Nonetheless, the most vital success factor in CPS is making sure time is committed to the creative process.

Conclusion

You will find different reasons for conflict. However, they could be distilled into the reality that everyone has unique mental models of how the world works. Such mental models are both efficient and inefficient. However, they are extremely useful in the way that they streamline everyone's lives. It also saves you the energy of having to rethink every single standpoint you have whenever you're confronted with a situation.

These mental models are all contextual. You have different models for every facet of life, from whom you decide to be friends with, to what type of music you listen to, to the types of food you and the model of the car you drive.

Now, let me ask you a question: what is your mental model? Which of these mental models are effective for you? Is it helping you? In what way?